G000122726

Greater Than a Tourist Book Series

I think the series is wonderful and beneficial for tourists to get information before visiting the city.

-Seckin Zumbul, Izmir Turkey

I am a world traveler who has read many trip guides but this one really made a difference for me. I would call it a heartfelt creation of a local guide expert instead of just a guide.

-Susy, Isla Holbox, Mexico

New to the area like me, this is a must have!

-Joe, Bloomington, USA

This is a good series that gets down to it when looking for things to do at your destination without having to read a novel for just a few ideas.

-Rachel, Monterey, USA

Good information to have to plan my trip to this destination.

-Pennie Farrell, Mexico

Aptly titled, you won't just be a tourist after reading this book. You'll be greater than a tourist!

-Alan Warner, Grand Rapids, USA

Thank you for a fantastic book.

-Don, Philadelphia, USA

Renee Schräder

Great ideas for a port day.
-Mary Martin USA

Even though I only have three days to spend in San Miguel in an upcoming visit, I will use the author's suggestions to guide some of my time there. An easy read - with chapters named to guide me in directions I want to go.
-Robert Catapano, USA

Great insights from a local perspective! Useful information and a very good value!
-Sarah, USA

This series provides an in-depth experience through the eyes of a local. Reading these series will help you to travel the city in with confidence and it'll make your journey a unique one.
-Andrew Teoh, Ipoh, Malaysia

Tourists can get an amazing "insider scoop" about a lot of places from all over the world. While reading, you can feel how much love the writer put in it.
-Vanja Živković, Sremski Karlovci, Serbia

GREATER THAN A TOURIST – ATITLÁN GUATEMALA

50 Travel Tips from a Local

Renee Schräder

Renee Schräder

Cover designed by Ivana Stamenkovic
Cover images: https://pixabay.com/en/atitlan-guatemala-logo-water-palms-912570/

Greater Than a Tourist
Visit our website at www.GreaterThanaTourist.com

Lock Haven, PA

ISBN: 9781980342175

>TOURIST

50 TRAVEL TIPS FROM A LOCAL

Renee Schräder

BOOK DESCRIPTION

Are you excited about planning your next trip?

Do you want to try something new?

Would you like some guidance from a local?

If you answered yes to any of these questions, then this Greater Than a Tourist book is for you.

Greater Than a Tourist – Atitlán, Guatemala by Renee Schräder offers the inside scope on the towns surrounding Lake Atitlán. Most travel books tell you how to travel like a tourist. Although there is nothing wrong with that, as part of the Greater Than a Tourist series, this book will give you travel tips from someone who has lived at your next travel destination.

In these pages, you will discover advice that will help you throughout your stay. This book will not tell you exact addresses or store hours but instead will give you excitement and knowledge from a local that you may not find in other smaller print travel books.

Travel like a local. Slow down, stay in one place, and get to know the people and the culture. By the time you finish this book, you will be eager and prepared to travel to your next destination.

Renee Schräder

TABLE OF CONTENTS

14. Learn how to cook traditional Guatemalan food from a local in San Pedro La Laguna

15. Find the cheapest accommodation in San Pedro La Laguna

16. Get customized shoes made on the streets of San Pedro La Laguna

17. Climb volcano San Pedro

18. Walk the hidden rocky shore of San Pedro La Laguna

19. Visit a little-known lookout point in San Pedro La Laguna

20. Photograph the sunrise in San Pedro La Laguna

21. Eat the pizza that will make you fall in love with vegan food in San Pedro La Laguna

22. Drink the best hot chocolate of your life in San Pedro La Laguna

23. Celebrate the Virgin Maria with the locals in San Pedro La Laguna

24. Climb the "Indian Nose" to see the sunrise

25. Visit a medicinal herbs and plants garden in San Juan La Laguna

26. Learn about organic coffee in San Juan La Laguna

27. Learn how traditional Guatemalan clothes are made in San Juan La Laguna

28. Admire some modern street art in San Juan La Laguna

29. Visit a nature reserve in San Marcos

30. Jump from 22 ft into the lake in San Marcos

31. Kayak around the lake

32. Find your zen in San Marcos

33. Try the best homemade nachos in San Marcos

34. Get a good feel of local life in Tzununa

35. Try simply delicious local food in Tzununa

36. Volunteer on an organic farm in Tzununa

37. Shop for handicrafts in Santiago

38. See the god that drinks alcohol and smokes cigarettes in Santiago
39. Take great street photos in Santiago
40. Learn about backstrap loom weaving in Santiago
41. Learn about permaculture from a local in San Lucas Tolimán
42. Dive into the depths of the lake from the shores of Santa Cruz La Laguna
43. Photograph the sunset in Panajachel
44. Learn about lake Atitlán's history in Museo Lacustre Atitlán
45. Try pupusas in Chero's Bar in Panajachel
46. See work from Guatemalan artists in La Galería in Panajachel
47. Take great pictures and eat great food in the Circus Bar in Panajachel
48. Eat the best breakfast crêpes of your life in Panajachel
49. Go to the beach in Panajachel
50. Visit the biggest market in Central America in Chichicastenango (from Panajachel)

Top Reasons to Book This Trip
> TOURIST
GREATER THAN A TOURIST
> TOURIST
GREATER THAN A TOURIST
NOTES

DEDICATION

To the people of Atitlán.

You have a unique gift in your possession; a mother in the form of an enchanting lake embraced by misty mountains and smoking volcanoes. Treasure her, like you would any mother, and tended you will be kept on her shores.

Renee Schräder

ABOUT THE AUTHOR

As a writer, photographer and filmmaker I have spent a year working in Guatemala on environment- and social justice related projects.

One of my environmental projects led me to live amongst the locals of San Pedro La Laguna, teaching me about the ancient culture and many traditions that find their home in lake Atitlán. Motivated to help the native residents better profit from the tourism at the lake and inspire more conscious tourism to this location and beyond, I wrote this book with the people in mind, and nature at heart.

- Renee Schräder

Renee Schräder

HOW TO USE THIS BOOK

The Greater Than a Tourist book series was written by someone who has lived in an area for over three months. The goal of this book is to help travelers either dream or experience different locations by providing opinions from a local. The author has made suggestions based on their own experiences. Please do your own research before traveling to the area in case the suggested places are unavailable.

Renee Schräder

FROM THE PUBLISHER

Traveling can be one of the most important parts of a person's life. The anticipation and memories that you have are some of the best. As a publisher of the Greater Than a Tourist book series, as well as the popular 50 Things to Know book series, we strive to help you learn about new places, spark your imagination, and inspire you. Wherever you are and whatever you do I wish you safe, fun, and inspiring travel.

Lisa Rusczyk Ed. D.
CZYK Publishing

Renee Schräder

OUR STORY

Traveling is a passion of the "Greater than a Tourist" series creator. Lisa studied abroad in college, and for their honeymoon Lisa and her husband toured Europe. During her travels to Malta, an older man tried to give her some advice based on his own experience living on the island since he was a young boy. She was not sure if she should talk to the stranger but was interested in his advice. When traveling to some places she was wary to talk to locals because she was afraid that they weren't being genuine. Through her travels, Lisa learned how much locals had to share with tourists. Lisa created the "Greater Than a Tourist" book series to help connect people with locals. A topic that locals are very passionate about sharing.

Renee Schräder

WELCOME TO
> TOURIST

Renee Schräder

INTRODUCTION

Although Guatemala has built a reputation of gangs and violence, the atmosphere around lake Atitlán will prove to be quite the opposite.

When approached as such, the locals dwelling in the surrounding lake towns are actually incredibly friendly and open, and have a lot of ancient knowledge to offer any listening ear.

This book is aimed at helping those visiting the lake to experience authentic, local life, and at giving a nudge in the direction of more conscious travel.

Renee Schräder

1. Choose locally-owned restaurants, hotels and activities

When visiting any of the towns around lake Atitlán, make it a priority to choose locally-owned hotels, hostels, restaurants, bars, tour companies, and language schools.

Although a significant amount of the mostly indigenous inhabitants of Atitlán have managed to find their way around profiting from lake Atitlán's quite recent tourism bloom, money earned from tourism does not always reach – let alone have a positive effect on – the local community and economy. So-called expats have settled in many of the lake's surrounding towns, and most of them own either hotels, restaurants, tour companies, or shops. Some of them do employ locals or give back in other ways, but many don't. Choosing any of these services would mean your dollars go right back to the western country you probably came from, instead of to the place you traveled all this way to visit and admire.

The locals in Atitlán – in entire Guatemala – have a lot to offer, and missing out on learning from this incredibly rich culture would be a waste of a potentially awe-inspiring trip! Most tips in this book are for locally-owned places and attractions, and if not they at least employ local staff or directly benefit the community in other ways.

Renee Schräder

2. Learn about and respect the local Mayan culture

The first thing to learn about the culture around lake Atitlán is the great importance most inhabitants give to the lake, or "their mother". Lake Atitlán – and water in general – is seen by the indigenous Maya as the giver of life, and is said to possess powerful cleansing and healing qualities.

When indigenous people from around the country visit lake Atitlán, the first thing they will do is dip their bare hands and feet into the water. This is not only a way to greet the lake, they believe it will also heal and purify them.

Rituals are held by Mayan healers to thank the lake for the life she provides. These are usually private and not meant to be a tourist attraction, but if you happen to befriend a Mayan healer and ask politely, he or she might just make an exception for you.

Another thing to take into account regarding the local culture is the fact that Guatemalan culture is one of amazing handicraft skills. So, when you go around shopping for those great textiles, baskets, woodworks, shoes – you name it, be mindful of who you buy from. There are many women weavers associations surrounding the lake, empowering women by selling their work and making sure the money ends up directly in their hands. Beware of machine-made fabrics – not only are they not authentic, the local craftswomen cannot compete with these lower prices and sometimes end up buying and re-selling the machine-made products instead of practicing their own ancient craft that plays such an important role in their culture.

3. The only footprint you leave should be in the sand

When visiting any location, but especially when going to a place considered sacred by its inhabitants, it is important to be mindful of the footprint you are leaving behind.

Lake Atitlán is one of the many lakes threatened with eutrophication (meaning the oxygen in the water is disappearing) as a consequence of heavy pollution, as well as biodiversity loss due to invasive species introduced by the United States and other western countries.

Of course, you probably won't be visiting the lake with your goldfish in your backpack, but you can prevent much of the pollution from entering the lake. A good way to reduce your waste would be bringing your own bags to the markets, along with some jars instead of plastic bags to store those kilos of beans. The market vendors will often have the option of wrapping their products in either leaves or paper, too, so ask for those when you see them reach for the plastic bags instead.

If you happen to buy some products in one of the tienditas that are already packed in plastic, make sure you dispose of the packaging correctly (you will probably not find any trash bins alongside the roads in most towns, so just hang on to your wrappers until you get back to your hotel).

When it comes to water, you could bring along your own reusable water bottle and refill it at your hostel (where they will probably have a water filter or Agua Pura). If you are in one of the bigger towns such as Panajachel, you can find places along the road where they will let you refill your water bottle too.

4. Get involved in local clean-ups

If you want to get more involved in the local community and help out the lake in the process, a good way to do this would be to participate in local clean-ups.

In most towns (San Pedro La Laguna especially) the fishermen and their families will get together every once in a while to clean up the shores and waters of the lake. They will most probably be very happy for you to join them – simply ask a fisherman when the next clean-up is, and if they would like some help. This is also a great way to get to know the surroundings of the lake like a local, and hear some of the numerous myths and stories that circle these waters.

Keep in mind that some of the elder locals might not speak a very clear Spanish, let alone English, because they will be native in their local tongue (Kaqchiquell, Tz'utujil, or K'iche, depending on your location). Don't let this stop you though, some broken Spanish and improvised sign language can get you a long way!

5. Learn your way around the lanchas crossing lake Atitlán

The very best way to get around lake Atitlán is by making use of the "lanchas", or boats, that depart regularly from the docks in every town. They are more efficient than taking a chicken bus, taxi, tuktuk or pickup from town to town, not to mention a whole lot safer. Although robberies and other problems on the road are not as common here as they are in most other parts of Guatemala, the roads are still best avoided whenever possible.

Luck does play a significant role in taking the lanchas, so stay sharp and don't expect to leave at a certain hour. Most boats will not leave until they are filled up or have at least 15 people. Best to just sit back, relax, and enjoy the view of the lake while you wait for more people to come. Sometimes this takes 3 minutes, sometimes 30, depending on the time of the day and day of the week.

If you are looking for a boat leaving from Panajachel, make sure to use the dock at the end of the street called Calle del Embarcadero. This is the dock most commonly used by the locals, and you'll be less likely to run into scams. If you do choose to use the other dock (at the end of Calle Santander), don't let them talk you into taking a private boat. Waiting hours are never as long as claimed, and public boats are the most common way of transportation for both locals and tourists.

6. Buy fresh fruits and vegetables on the markets

By far the best way to eat well and eat cheap in Atitlán is by buying fresh products on the markets. There are countless fruits and vegetables to be found in the stands every day, as well as freshly-made tortillas and chuchitos, meat sliced from what seems like half the cow hanging right in front of you, and every single part of the chicken (chicken feet with chicken brain, anyone?).

Although not all of those options might be appealing to everyone, do not shy away from fruits or vegetables that you don't know. When in season (between July and October), try out the famous Guatemalan jocotes. These little oval fruits can be found in yellow, red or green, and are often eaten unripe by the locals, served with some salt. They are said to prefer quite tart and bitter foods, so if that is not your thing try these fruits out when their colors are very bright – this means they are very ripe. Their taste hangs somewhere between sweet and sour, and vaguely reminds one of a tiny, more sour mango.

7. Have your breakfast in the streets

Street food for breakfast? Why not! Many locals in the towns surrounding the lake will eat their breakfast either on the market or on the streets, where stands can be found selling hot cereals or tostadas with drinks such as rosa de Jamaica (a cold hibiscus tea), horchata (a traditional sweet rice drink) or fresh lemonade.

The tostadas can be made up to your own liking, and toppings will usually include guacamole, refried beans, some queso seco (dry cheese) and a chicken-based paste. What exactly makes up the hot cereals is still somewhat of a mystery to me. What I do know is that it usually contains any or all kinds of cereal, hot milk, and I've even seen people mix some Cheetos in there...

8. Eat chuchitos from the market

After learning that a dog was often referred to as chucho, I was slightly shocked when I was invited to try some chuchitos. But, not to worry, the only meat found in these corn leave-wrapped packages is chicken, clearly distinguishable from dog...

The chuchito is a staple at most markets in Guatemala, best bought in the mornings when they're still hot. They're made of a mass of corn, and traditionally filled with a little piece of chicken and tomato-based sauce. Some might contain chiles too, so make sure to ask for a chile-free one if you're not into spicy breakfasts!

Chuchitos come wrapped in the leaves of corn, and often the vendors will wrap a bigger banana leave around them for transport. You can eat them straight out of the leave, or take them home to enjoy alongside a traditional breakfast of tortillas, fried plantain and refried beans. Don't miss out on them if you are a vegetarian, either. The little piece of chicken is easily taken out, and any street dog will happily take care of it for you.

9. Hunt for Tamales on the markets

The tamale could be seen as the big brother of the chuchito. Bigger, square and usually wrapped in a banana leave, this traditional dish knows many varieties.

The tamale originates in neighboring Mexico, but Guatemala has made this dish their own by excelling in an impressive number of varieties. The most common ones are the tamales de gallina – a corn dough filled with some chicken and a tomato-based sauce. Other varieties could have a rice-based dough instead, or hold different meats, sardines, prunes, red bell peppers, olives or raisins.

Although very similar to the chuchito, tamales are considered to be for special occasions and festivities, such as birthdays or Christmas. Unwrapping the tamale is like opening a gift, the locals say, so finding these presents on a regular weekday on the markets will be a challenge. Take your best chances by coming very early, when the stands are still being set up, and ask around. If you are lucky, there will be a local woman or two selling some fresh tamales.

10. Roam the streets at night for some great BBQ

If you're a meat eater and have already stuffed yourself to the maximum with fresh fruits, vegetables and tortillas, roam the streets in the evening to find some great BBQ-ing. Simply follow your nose and it will take you to one of the many stands that seem pop up anywhere from the late afternoon onward.

Food served ranges from tacos to platos fuertes ("strong plates", so basically a big meal), with options of grilled chicken, beef or pork. Also be sure to look out for elotes, a white corn that is cooked on the BBQ and then eaten with some lime and salt – as delicious as it is simple.

Don't be too afraid to eat street food, just follow the simple rules: eat things that are hot from the fire, and choose stands that are busy with locals (they wouldn't be coming back there if the food was bad).

11. Visit a Mayan Healer in San Pedro La Laguna

For a real immersion in lake Atitlán and its culture, try to arrange a visit with a Mayan healer.

The art of healing is often passed on from generation to generation, and modern healers still possess much of the ancient Mayan wisdom. At certain times they might hold rituals, some of which involve honoring lake Atitlán, which they believe to be the giver of life.

Visiting a Mayan ritual is not a tourist attraction, and unless you are genuinely interested in learning about the Mayas and their culture it is probably best to stick to chatting with the locals instead. If you do possess that genuine interest, you can ask one of the tour companies to put you in touch with a Mayan healer. The tour company on your right hand side when just arriving at the dock of San Pedro La Laguna has a list with contact information of Mayan healers from the town as well as some from the neighboring town San Juan.

Don't expect to be invited along with sacred rituals right away - instead, be satisfied with a meeting with a healer and simply talk with them about what it is interests you about the Mayan culture. Then, if you ask politely, you might be invited to the next ritual.

12. Brush up on your Spanish in San Pedro La Laguna

Practically all towns surrounding lake Atitlán have at least one Spanish language school, and for good reason – who wouldn't want to take their Spanish lessons sitting by the lake, with a view of the volcanos?

To take full advantage of this perfect location, opt for Casa Rosario Spanish School in San Pedro La Laguna. Their classes are all one-on-one, taught by locals who have a perfect understanding of English as well as Spanish. The best part is, you won't be spending your days studying in a classroom. Instead, little huts and tree houses have been built in a garden with trees and stretches of grass, separated from the lake only by a couple of rocks. That means studying in the cool shade with a warm breeze between the pages of your books, and taking study-breaks by dipping your toes into the cool blue water… What more could you wish for?

13. Learn to speak the ancient Mayan language of Tz'utujil in San Pedro La Laguna

Should your Spanish already be on point, you could still pick up some new language skills in San Pedro La Laguna. Right next to the church and central park, a little road will lead you to a language institution. They teach the ancient Mayan language of Tz'utujil and do professional translating work as well, should you happen to be in need of some very accurate translating or interpreting.

This language school is not exactly aimed at tourists, and a good level of Spanish is required if you want to be able to understand the teachers and/or translators – most of them do not speak English.

14. Learn how to cook traditional Guatemalan food from a local in San Pedro La Laguna

If you want to try your hand at cooking some delicious Guatemalan food, sign up for a cooking class with Anita from Mayan Kitchen in San Pedro La Laguna. She has by far the best cooking classes in

Atitlán, if not in the country, and can teach in Spanish or English (or two out of three of the local Mayan languages, if you wish…).

Your day of cooking will start with a trip to the market, where you will pick up all the fresh ingredients needed to make your traditional Mayan meal. Once all ingredients have been collected, Anita will invite you into her kitchen where she will explain all the details of the special recipe, the history and background story of the dish, some do's and don'ts, and anything else you might want to know. Once the meal is cooked and ready you will enjoy it with Anita and the other students, after which there is the opportunity to visit the women weavers co-op that Anita started.

This cooking class will teach you far more about the Mayan culture and customs than any of the museums ever could; I highly recommend it.

15. Find the cheapest accommodation in San Pedro La Laguna

San Pedro La Laguna is by far the most affordable town to stay in. Hostels, hotels and even Airbnb locations are a lot cheaper in this town than most others, which might in part be due to its reputation of the "party town". However, once you look past the main tourist's street with its party hostels, there is actually quite a lot of quiet space to be found in San Pedro La Laguna where you can relax without any party-esque disturbances.

A great way to find a cheap stay in San Pedro La Laguna – and any of the towns, really – is by strolling around in search of local hotels. Many are quite old-fashioned and will not have an online presence, and their rates are often the lowest in town.

If you want some more privacy and are staying for a long period of time, the same tactic can work for finding a budget-friendly place to rent. Bungalows and apartments are often rented out cheap, announced simply by a paper with a phone number on the door. Be on the lookout for these as you roam the streets, and you might stumble upon a great bargain.

16. Get customized shoes made on the streets of San Pedro La Laguna

When coming up from the main dock into San Pedro, take the first road on your left to find a small stand selling unique, high-quality leather shoes and bags. The owner and creator of these incredible crafts is called Pedro, and he will make (or repair) custom leather shoes and handbags for very friendly prices.

To find him, it might take a little more than asking around for Pedro (as practically half the men in town are named Pedro). Asking for the man that makes shoes and bags might get you a bit further, and if you don't happen to find him with his stand ask in the shop that makes fancy leather backpacks at the other end of the street. He is usually there in the afternoons, so your best luck of running into him will be after 2 P.M. Getting items custom-made will take a couple of days, so try to find him in the early days of your Atitlán stay!

17. Climb volcano San Pedro

For the more adventurous traveler, an epic volcano climb is only a short tuktuk ride away from the dock of San Pedro La Laguna. While volcano San Pedro is not the highest one in the Atitlán region, with 9,908ft it still towers high above the lake. The views from this volcano are absolutely spectacular, even – or especially – on cloudy days. A thick carpet of clouds stretches out for miles around you on those grey days, giving you the illusion of standing on top of the clouds. On clear days the view of the lake and surrounding volcanoes is just as spectacular.

To climb the volcano you need to follow the road that leads to Santiago, and enter a natural park. Make sure to go with a local guide – going without will just get you lost on a cold volcano top, and you will not even safe any money in the process because an entrance fee will be charged for those hiking without a guide. Guides can be found in practically all of the tour companies crowding the main streets of San Pedro La Laguna.

18. Walk the hidden rocky shore of San Pedro La Laguna

For a slightly less strenuous walk that will still get you far away from the hustle and bustle of the crowds, go and explore las piedras, or the rocks; a great place to clear your head or take some stunning pictures.

When you arrive at the main dock of San Pedro La Laguna, follow the main road to the left, until the end. There, a small, unofficial path will lead you to a rocky trail lined with flowers and enormous trees, ending at the very tip of San Pedro's shore. Don't be afraid to get lost, there is practically only one way to go.

I recommend climbing up and down the rocks on both sides of the trail; going down next to the water will reveal new sights of the lake and its surrounding, and climbing up on your right will provide a bird's view-look at the town and its stacked-up houses and meandering streets.

19. Visit a little-known lookout point in San Pedro La Laguna

On the road to Santiago from San Pedro La Laguna, a short while before the entrance to the natural park leading up to the volcano, there is a little-known lookout place that offers marvelous views of lake Atitlán and some of the mountain ranges.

Ask a tuktuk driver to take you up to the closest mirador, and ask him to wait for you while you enjoy the view (not that many tuktuks pass here, so best to hold on to the one you have). You will be driven up to the house of some very smart and business-oriented locals, who have used their house's location to their advantage and built a wooden lookout in their backyard. The entrance fee is only a few Quetzales per person, and great photographs can be taken from the top. Don't forget to thank the locals when you leave, and greet the pet bunnies on your way out.

Renee Schräder

20. Photograph the sunrise in San Pedro La Laguna

For all (aspiring) photographers visiting the lake: San Pedro La Laguna is the place to be to capture an enchanting sunrise from behind the volcanos.

My personal favorite spot to photograph the sun taking its first look at Atitlán is from the Santiago dock, located at the end of the street that leads down from the market. I recommend getting there early – very early – to get a glimpse of the great moon-lit sky before it starts turning pink, orange and blue. The sun will rise close to cerro de oro (in case you want to set your camera up for a time-lapse), but don't ignore the rest of the landscape either; the morning light will shape and color everything in a way fit for illustrations of a fairytale.

21. Eat the pizza that will make you fall in love with vegan food in San Pedro La Laguna

If you're on the hunt for a delicious lunch that does not contain beans or tortillas, you could change it up and visit the vegetarian restaurant called The 5th Dimension. Located in the main street (taking a right from the main dock), this little restaurant offers some incredible meat-free options.

Dishes range from burritos and pizzas to salads and smoothies, all vegetarian with many vegan options available. The prices are a little bit higher than most other restaurants in San Pedro, but still very competitive and definitely western budget-friendly. I personally recommend the pizzas – even if you are a meat-lover at heart, this pizza will definitely win you over and make you forget about the existence of salami and cheese for a moment.

22. Drink the best hot chocolate of your life in San Pedro La Laguna

In my humble opinion, drinking hot chocolate in Guatemala that is not made from raw cacao is a sin. You are in a country filled with amazing natural ingredients – don't accept a drink of the gods made from powders (same goes for coffee).

To make sure you don't accidentally sin and have to rush to the confession booth, take your coffee or hot chocolates in café Cristalinas, located on your left hand side on the hill going straight up from the main dock. I've been told people drink the best cup of coffee of their life here, and myself being more of a chocolate person, I can say the same is true for the hot chocolate. For lactose-intolerant or vegan guests the drink can be made with soy- or almond milk upon request.

The coffee and cacao used in this café is all locally sourced from several small farms in the region, and while you sip your drink some coffee plants can be spotted growing at the end of the terrace. Fresh coffee beans can be bought at the counter, too, and don't pass up the opportunity to try some of their home-made carrot cake or banana bread to go with your hot cup of goodness.

23. Celebrate the Virgin Maria with the locals in San Pedro La Laguna

If you happen to find yourself in San Pedro La Laguna on the 8th of December, keep your evening schedule free and make your way up to the parque municipal. A celebration in honor of the virgin Maria will be taking place in the way of excessive fireworks, tacos from street stands and a local band singing (religious) songs at every street corner, all while a procession with a statue of the holy virgin marches through the streets of the town.

If you've already befriended some locals, invite them to go together as they will probably be able to explain you a bit more of the story behind the celebration. Also make sure to stay until the end, when the holy virgin and accompanying procession make their way back to the church, and a final spectacle of fireworks will seal the evening.

24. Climb the "Indian Nose" to see the sunrise

This 9,393 ft-high mountain can easily be recognized from the town of San Juan and San Pedro because of its resemblance to a face in profile, referred to as the "Indian Nose".

To climb this huge face, prepare to get out of bed timely, as tours will leave as early as 4 in the morning. The result is definitely worth it though, as your ascend will be rewarded with a stunning view of the lake and its volcanoes. You will be able to watch the sun shed its first rays of light of the day on the lake's tranquil waters, and look out over the awakening towns at the lake's shore from far above.

This hike definitely promises some of the best views over lake Atitlán, so be sure to charge your camera and free up plenty of memory space – once you start, you won't be able to stop taking pictures.

25. Visit a medicinal herbs and plants garden in San Juan La Laguna

Ancient Mayan wisdom can be found in many aspects of local life, one of them being medicine. Visiting a Mayan healer is one way to get a glimpse of this vast knowledge, visiting the Tza'an Ab'aaj garden

50m left of the dock in San Juan is another. The garden is owned by an elder local, who practices organic agriculture on his land and gives tours of all his medicinal plants and herbs.

Tours usually cost more or less the same as a meal in a local restaurant, and odds are you and whoever comes with you will be the only people in the tour. This creates opportunity for very interesting conversations with the owner, so be ready to fire away with any medicinal plant-related questions you might have.

26. Learn about organic coffee in San Juan La Laguna

Odds are you usually start your day with a cup of coffee, but actually have no clue where it came from or how it was grown, harvested and processed. In Atitlán you will have the opportunity to defy those odds, and learn everything you could possible want to know about coffee.

La Voz is an organic coffee farm located in San Juan that offers tours year round. Most harvesting is done from November through January, but visiting in other times of the year will still prove interesting. The entire growing process is organic, and you will learn all there is to know about this high altitude, shade-grown coffee and what exactly makes it taste so great. The farm supports local farming, and most people working here will actually own a piece of the land with which they are able to sustain their families.

27. Learn how traditional Guatemalan clothes are made in San Juan La Laguna

The most recognizable form of art in Guatemala can be found in the traditional, hand-woven clothes. Colorful wrap-around skirts and blouses (huipiles) with elaborated designs adorn most indigenous Mayan women, and some of the (mostly older) men will also still wear their traditional striped trousers and multi-colored blouses.

To learn how these incredible clothes are made, visit the Women Weavers Cooperative in San Juan. They can explain the complete process of backstrap weaving, from forming and naturally coloring the thread and mapping out the design to weaving and sewing together the final piece. A weaving demonstration will most certainly be given as well. In the shop, a tag with the name of the woman that created the piece will be attached to each item, and the women will be able to better support their family with the money they make from their craft.

28. Admire some modern street art in San Juan La Laguna

In the center of San Juan you will find a basketball field that doubles as the main event venue. Though not exactly a day trip, the art adorning the walls of this locale are worth a short visit.

The paintings tell the tale of a Mayan legend, and if a local happens to be roaming the same spot they will probably be happy to explain the story to you. Similar paintings can be found around this town and others too, so be on the lookout and spot them all!

29. Visit a nature reserve in San Marcos

If you want to spend some time soaking up the natural beauty of lake Atitlán's shores, visit the Cerro Tzankujil nature reserve located in San Marcos. The reserve borders the rocky shores of the lake, and well-kept trails will lead you through a forest of enormous trees, along the waters and up the hill.

When following the trails up, you will find a Mayan altar that is still used regularly by locals to perform rituals, give gratitude and ask for prosperity from their Mayan gods. Further up the hill, several stunning views of the lake are waiting to be taken in, as well as a great view of San Marcos from above.

This park is great for landscape photography, and will provide opportunity for shooting the lake from some of its most flattering angles. A small fee will be charged upon entrance, but after paying you are welcome to leave and come back any time during that day.

30. Jump from 22 ft into the lake in San Marcos

Once you've hiked to all the outskirts of the park, there is the option of dipping your toe in the clear blue waters. San Marcos is said to be one of the best towns for swimming, the water being more clear here compared to the shores of other towns. You can follow some of the smaller trails down the rocks to the water, or take a more adventurous route.

Located alongside the left side trail of the park, a platform hovers 22 ft above the lake. Many a thrill-seeker has taken a leap of fate into the waters here, so if you're the kind of person that likes to spend sunny afternoons jumping from cliffs, soaring with adrenaline – this place will allow you to do just that.

31. Kayak around the lake

Renting a kayak is an excellent way to explore the lake and spend some time in the peace and quiet of nature. A one- or two- person kayaks can be rented from most towns surrounding the lake for a small per-hour fee.

You could choose to rent your kayak for a couple of hours and make your way around the lake, or just get your little barge for 30 minute and bobber around while enjoying the sunshine. A great way to either get a tan or some exercise, whichever you prefer.

Make sure to avoid the strongest hours of the sun, which are more or less from 11AM until 3PM If you plan to stay out on the water for a longer time, it's best to set off early in the morning or later in the afternoon.

32. Find your zen in San Marcos

San Marcos is probably the best place to be around the lake for aspiring yogis. The town is crowded with health shops and meditation centers, and yoga getaways are a staple for pretty much any traveler visiting this town.

One of the most popular meditation centers, Las Pirámides, is located just on the left when coming up from the main dock. The center offers spiritual guidance in a place of natural tranquility, and a one-month personal development course can be followed, starting every full moon.

Renee Schräder

33. Try the best homemade nachos in San Marcos

Just left of the main square in San Marcos, a little restaurant called Moonfish can be found hiding away behind green vegetation. This is one of the best and most affordable places to eat vegan or vegetarian around the lake, and even if you normally like your big burgers with fries, this place is worth a try.

The fresh, homemade and locally grown food is very affordable, and ranges from burritos and sandwiches to tofu scrambles and tempeh dishes. I highly recommend trying their nachos with frijoles; the nachos are homemade, still smoking hot when served and absolutely delicious.

The staff is made up mostly of local women, and a friendly dog and cat or two will stroll around amongst the tables to see if you might drop some of your burrito on the floor. Great if a small pack of street dogs has already started following you; your new friends will be allowed to dine with you here without objection.

34. Get a good feel of local life in Tzununa

To get a better feel of what local life around the lake is like without the crowds of tourist interfering with your authentic experience, visit a smaller town such as Tzununa. This village is still quite untouched by tourism, although it is slowly starting to gain popularity.

The main road of the town goes up quite steep, which makes for stunning views of the lake practically every step you turn around to look at it. Further up, next to Hotel Bambú, a bridge goes over one of the few rivers flowing into lake Atitlán, and local women can often be seen washing their clothes on the rocks of the river bank.

If you happen to be staying in San Marcos, Tzununa is only a short boat ride away and makes for a nice day trip. It could also be reached by tuktuk, but this option is more expensive than taking a lancha.

35. Try simply delicious local food in Tzununa

To enhance the feeling of emersion in local life even more, have a taste of the simple, local cuisine at one of the few restaurants to be found in Tzununa. Up the road from the dock on your left hand side you will find a little sign simply announcing "restaurant Tzununa". Some stairs will lead you up to a terrace, where a few tables clad with locally-made table cloths stand in front of the breathtaking view.

Renee Schräder

Simply ask what dish is being served that day, and make sure to mention any dietary preferences. The simultaneous greatness and simplicity of this food will remind you of what a home-cooked meal is supposed to taste like.

36. Volunteer on an organic farm in Tzununa

Learn permaculture from experience by volunteering on an organic farm located on the outskirts of Panamá. Shad, the owner of the farm, is the kind of guy that ends his emails with "Pee outside!", just to give you an idea of what you're in for before you enter the world of permaculture on the lush green hills of Tzununa. Atitlán Organics is all about self-sustainability and making the most of a relatively small slope of land. Shad and his staff will teach you everything you could possibly want to know about permaculture, whether you have come to volunteer for a couple of weeks or just dropped by for the weekly farm tour.

If you want to volunteer, look up Atitlán Organics online, or get in touch with Shad through sites such as Workaway. Lodging is provided at a discounted price at Hotel Bambú, and a wonderful home-cooked meal will be waiting for you every day that you volunteer.

37. Shop for handicrafts in Santiago

The people of Guatemala seem to all have a gift for creating beautiful crafts with any material you put in front of them. Consequently, many tourist-oriented markets and souvenir shops crowd the towns surrounding the lake, and all seem to offer a variety of the same kind of craft. To find the most variety and choice within the lake towns, opt for a visit to Santiago.

Being the biggest town around the lake, it is not surprising that the many stands and souvenir shops bordering the (relatively) busy street leading to the dock offer a great variety of crafts. Items range from shoes, handbags and clothes to woodwork, woven baskets and jewelry. Make sure you choose handmade items over machine-made ones to support the local crafts, and don't haggle the price down too much; locals tend to charge very little already for crafts that might take weeks or months to complete. You can recognize handmade items from machine-made ones by little "imperfections" in the designs and the uniqueness of each peace.

Renee Schräder

38. See the god that drinks alcohol and smokes cigarettes in Santiago

To see a small spectacle you will not soon forget, ask around for Maximón (pronounced mah-shee-mohn) when in Santiago. This town has the unique custom of giving offerings and taking care of this holy image; a god embodied by a doll-like figure that thrives on alcohol, money and cigarettes.

Maximón is ceremonially moved to a new house every year after Semana Santa, and is taken care of by a family by being offered alcohol, cigarettes, and money - yes, they literally pour alcohol into the mouth of Maximón, and light him a cigarette while they humbly ask him to bring prosperity to a family business, health to a dear friend, or love for a family member.

You can simply find out Maximón's whereabouts by asking around in the street. Most probably somebody will take you and explain a bit more about the custom, after which they will expect to be tipped a small amount for their services.

39. Take great street photos in Santiago

Santiago is a relatively large and busy town, with crowded streets that have a bit more traffic going on than most other towns (Panajachel being the only exception). Unlike Panajachel, the other "big" town around the lake, Santiago is not constantly flooded with tourists coming from all over the world as well as from different parts of Guatemala. Because of this, locals tend to be a little less taken aback by yet another camera hanging from a tourist's neck.

In my experience, Santiago is one of the best towns for street photography. People are generally friendly, not too camera shy and will happily have their picture taken if you ask politely. Overall, men are a lot less taken aback by being requested to star in a street portrait than women, who are not that used to being the center of attention as they live in a culture where men still very much hold the reins.

40. Learn about backstrap loom weaving in Santiago

Chances are that if you visit more than one town around the lake, you'll notice subtle differences in the huipiles (blouses) and skirts of the indigenous women. In Panajachel and Santa Cruz you will find many soft, warm fabrics and colors as well as turban-like adornments, whereas San Pedro traditionally is represented by blue huipiles with wide, white collars.

To learn more about the traditional clothing of Guatemala and the weaving process behind it, you can visit the Cojolya Association of Women Weavers in Santiago. This museum asks only for a small donation upon entry, and in return will teach you everything there is to know about the history of the backstrap loom weaving craft through several displays and demonstrations. The entire process will be taken into account, and you will walk away with a whole new appreciation for the traditional Guatemalan clothing. The museum can be found on Calle Real, Santiago.

41. Learn about permaculture from a local in San Lucas Tolimán

Although not as easily reached as most other places around the lake, San Lucas Tolimán is worth the trouble of a visit for all those interested in learning about permaculture. Roni Lec, an indigenous resident of the Atitlán area and co-founder of a local organization called IMAP (the Mesoamerican Permaculture Institute), currently runs the whole operation and can be reached out to for lectures and courses on everything permaculture-related.

Being a native to the Atitlán area, Lec combines ancient Mayan (farming) knowledge with modern agriculture practices, using the best of both worlds to his advantage to develop sustainable solutions to conventional farming issues – which in turn will have a positive effect on the health of both the environment as well as all beings living in it. To learn at IMAP, simply visit their website and inform about upcoming courses and/or visits to the sustainable permaculture farm located in San Lucas Tolimán.

42. Dive into the depths of the lake from the shores of Santa Cruz La Laguna

To explore the depths of lake Atitlán more closely, visit ATI Divers in Santa Cruz la Laguna. Atitlán is one of the very few places where you can dive at altitude without wearing a wetsuit, so if that sounds like an opportunity perfect for you, do not pass it up while you're there.

ATI Atitlán offers a PADI high altitude course as well as a PADI open-water certification course, but just in case you are already experienced in these areas, they also offer guided dives into the lake. Because of the eruptive history of the lake, the underwater landscape is quite odd and impressive. To make the best of your diving trip, try to avoid diving in the rainy season (as the water will cloud up). The best time to visit for diving purposes is between October and May.

43. Photograph the sunset in Panajachel

Although Panajachel does not exactly have the reputation of being the town with the most green areas, the location is great for photographing the lake, especially during sunset.

If you visit the little beach located some way left of the dock, you will find a great view of Cerro de Oro and volcanoes Tolimán and San

Pedro behind the waters. This location is great for photographing the sunset, as the sun will set a little ways to the right from the volcanoes and color the sky and waters in many shades of pink and orange. Some fishermen will most probably be at work close to this location, too, providing a nice extra element in the form of silhouettes in your pictures.

44. Learn about lake Atitlán's history in Museo Lacustre Atitlán

To inform yourself on the history of lake Atitlán, a visit can be paid to Museo Lacustre Atitlán, hidden inside hotel Posada de Don Rodrigo. The museum shares information on the enormous volcanic eruptions that led to the creation of the lake, and practically every event after that.

Worthy sights include the ancients Mayan artifacts that have been collected from the depths of the lake, giving a glimpse of the civilization that once threaded the volcanic earth surrounding the waters. Adding to this experience is the display of the (relatively) recently discovered Mayan ceremonial center, Samabaj, located on the bottom of the lake near Cerro de Oro.

45. Try pupusas in Chero's Bar in Panajachel

Although traditionally a Salvadorian dish, pupusas can be found throughout Guatemala as well. The best way to describe a pupusa to someone who has never tried one before would be to say it is a somewhat thicker, usually cheese-filled tortilla, served with a side of pickled cabbage and salsa.

The owner of the place seems to be well-known and respected by practically everyone in town, so don't be surprised if many a local will pop by to say hi, followed by groups of working people on their lunch break, suited men out on business lunches and a tourist or two who knew just where to be for a delicious, affordable lunch.

The food is cooked behind the bar right before your eyes, and it will cost you barely anything. Opt for a standard cheese and refried beans-filled pupusa if you want to play it safe, or try more exotic varieties containing spinach, chipilín, or albahaca to spice things up.

If you are a vegan or vegetarian, do try out Chero's, too – many pupusas don't contain meat and any variety can be made cheese-free upon request.

46. See work from Guatemalan artists in La Galería in Panajachel

Guatemalan culture doesn't begin and end with ancient weaving skills. Many talented artists have roamed this country (or currently do), and indigenous painter Nan Cuz felt it time to exhibit their work. He founded La Galería in 1971, displaying artwork exclusively from Guatemalan painters and sculptures.

Nowadays the exhibition can still be visited, and on occasion lectures, film screenings, or concerts will be held at this venue. The gallery can be found on Calle Rancho Grande, and entry is free of charge – no reasons to miss out on this little piece of (well-deserved) national pride!

Renee Schräder

47. Take great pictures and eat great food in the Circus Bar in Panajachel

For the photographers that like to utilize the time spent waiting for their food for taking some shots, the circus bar in Panajachel is the place to be. The restaurant is somewhat pricier than Chero's bar, for example, but the food is great and entering the themed restaurant is an experience in itself.

Needless to say, the circus Bar is completely circus-themed, with old pictures of circus days past decorating the walls, and an old piano adorned with some clowns' shoes and top hat occupying a big part of a tiny stage meant for live music (occurring nightly) – even entering the bathroom feels like entering a (very private) circus tent. The light is quite dim and aids perfectly in taking dramatic photos of the venue while you wait for your choice of the wide array of dishes.

48. Eat the best breakfast crêpes of your life in Panajachel

On days where a quick, affordable meal with a home-cooked quality is desired, Los Almendros is the place to retire to. Located on Calle Santander in Panajachel, this tiny café is a popular eating and meeting place for tourists, locals, and expats alike. Breakfast can (and in my opinion, should) be ordered all day, and daily specials will run for prices lower than a soda will cost you in a western country.

The food is prepared right in front of you, at the bar located between the table-lined terrace and little supermarket. If you want to indulge in an incredible, sweet breakfast, I recommend the crêpes above all else – you'll walk away with a lingering feeling that you just ate the best crêpes of your life, and no fancy French bistro could compete. You might also feel like you won't be able to fit any other food into your system for the rest of the day, which I just like to look at as a nice money-saving bonus.

49. Go to the beach in Panajachel

With Panajachel functioning as a portal between lake Atitlán and the rest of the world, the town can get quite busy with tourists and passers-through. To get away from this noise and find some peace and quiet while taking in the breathtaking views of the lake and its mountains, visit the little beach tucked away left of the main dock. Simply follow the road next to the shore to the left, and don't stop when the road does; simply continue onward until you pass River Panajachel followed by abandoned stands and huts. Behind this, you will find many locals relaxing on a little beach and enjoying the cool water of the lake. Join them, take a breath, relax in the afternoon sun, and make sure to stick around until 6 P.M. to enjoy the sunset.

50. Visit the biggest market in Central America in Chichicastenango (from Panajachel)

When visiting the lake, schedule a visit to the market in Chichicastenango on a Thursday or Sunday morning. Located more or less an hour away from the lake, Chichicastenango holds one of the biggest markets in Central America, and has grown to be a great tourist attraction.

Some villagers still travel for many hours carrying their products on their backs and heads to sell at the Chichi market, but a lot of vendors are also located in Chichicastenango. Endless rows of tourist-oriented stalls crowd the streets, selling clothes, shoes, textiles, pottery, and other handicrafts bearing the traditional colorful patterns of Guatemala.

In the north of the square a more local crowd can be found shopping for their everyday needs, such as food, clothes, soaps, etc. This area also offers great photo opportunities, but do be polite and ask locals for permission before you snap their picture.

Renee Schräder

Top Reasons to Book This Trip

- **Ancient cultures:** Very little countries have managed to hold on to so much of their traditional cultures despite being invaded and colonized. Atitlán is one of the best places in the world to experience and learn from the incredibly rich Mayan culture that is still very much alive today.

- **Stunning locale:** To say lake Atitlán looks impressive, with its numerous volcanoes, mountain sides and blue waters, would be the understatement of understatements. The mere sight of this beautiful portrait painted by mother nature is worth the trouble of the trip to this location.

- **Guatemalan cuisine:** Although far from internationally recognized, Guatemala holds some incredibly delicious national recipes that capture every taste in their complicated simplicity.

- **Humanity:** Participation in local life in the towns surrounding lake Atitlán reminds you of what life amongst fellow humans is supposed to feel like; a sense of warmth, hospitality and togetherness hovers over the simple houses, and to even temporarily form a part of that will make you feel right at home.

Renee Schräder

> TOURIST
GREATER THAN A TOURIST

Visit GreaterThanATourist.com:
http://GreaterThanATourist.com

Sign up for the Greater Than a Tourist Newsletter:
http://eepurl.com/cxspyf

Follow us on Facebook:
https://www.facebook.com/GreaterThanATourist

Follow us on Pinterest:
http://pinterest.com/GreaterThanATourist

Follow us on Instagram:
http://Instagram.com/GreaterThanATourist

Renee Schräder

> TOURIST
GREATER THAN A TOURIST

Please leave your honest review of this book on Amazon and Goodreads. Thank you. We appreciate your positive and constructive feedback. Thank you.

Renee Schräder

NOTES

Printed in Great Britain
by Amazon

16927448R00046